TRANSLATED BY DAVID HENRY WILSON

HEINZ JANISCH   MAJA KASTELIC

Hans Christian Andersen

THE JOURNEY OF HIS LIFE

North
South

"The most wonderful fairy tale is life itself."
HANS CHRISTIAN ANDERSEN

"Are you old?"

"Darling, you mustn't ask the gentleman such a question!"

"You must forgive my daughter. She's only a child."

"I like children who ask questions," said the man with a friendly smile.
"I'm always pleased to meet inquisitive children."
He turned toward the girl, who was wearing a crisp blue dress.

"You wanted to know if I'm old. Well, yes. I'm as young as the boy that I once was and can still feel inside me. And I'm as old as the man who is sitting opposite you."

"Then you're young *and* you're old," said the girl, a little surprised.
"I suppose I am," said the man.

"My name is Elsa. I'm seven."

"I'm looking forward to Copenhagen, where we're going. I've even brought a book about Copenhagen with me. Do you like reading too?"

"Pleased to meet you. And my name is Hans Christian Andersen. I'm honored to be sharing this coach with you and your mother."

"I like it a lot. And I also like writing. In fact, writing is my job."

Elsa looked at him in amazement. "Do you mean you write real books?"

"I write stories that sometimes get published. And I particularly like telling fairy tales."

Elsa's eyes lit up. "I love fairy tales! Will you tell me one now?"

The coach drove over a bump, and the travelers were given a good shaking.
The sky-blue dress rustled.

The man bent forward.

"I could tell you a very special fairy story," he said.

"Which one?"

"If you like, I'll tell you the story of a boy who learned to fly."
"I'd like to hear that," said Elsa eagerly.
The man who had introduced himself as Hans Christian Andersen cleared his throat and began his story.

"Once upon a time there was a boy who from the very beginning had a really tough life. In other words, his childhood was full of great big holes through which there blew a very cold, wild wind.

"He was born on an island that belonged to Denmark.
By the way, did you know that there are 483 islands in Denmark?"
Elsa shook her head.

"The boy's name was Hans. Sometimes an old man
used to go round the place where he lived selling
wooden figures that he'd carved himself.

"He had flowers in his hat and sang strange songs.

"This white-haired old man was Hans's grandfather. The stresses and strains of life had made him a bit peculiar. And life was very stressful in those days.

"There was little to eat, and many people went hungry.
You had to be grateful if there was some sort of work for you to do, even if you didn't get paid much for it.

"Hans's father was a cobbler. He patched the holes in people's shoes. There were always piles of old shoes on the floor of his workshop. And the workshop was also the living room and bedroom for the whole family.

"The father would sit on a little wooden chair from morning till evening, but the pile of shoes with holes in them just refused to get any smaller.

"In the evening, he would push the pile of shoes to one side and then—after a bowl of thin soup and a piece of bread—he would take out a big book of fairy tales.
"The father would read out loud, and Hans, his son, would listen entranced, his cheeks glowing with excitement.
"Hans's mother also liked to listen.

"The fairy tales told of a magical world in which anything was possible.

"It told of princesses and princes, of queens and kings, and of strange and wonderful happenings....

"Another magical world was the puppet theater that Hans's father had built for him.
Hans's father had even made clothes for the puppets, and on some evenings he would act out a story that
he had made up for Hans.

"It's hardly surprising
that later in his life
Hans himself wrote
plays and stories in which
anything was possible.
His father's book of
fairy tales had given him
wings, and so,
thanks to all the stories,
he had learned to fly!

"One day Hans's father became a soldier and went to war.
He thought that afterward he might be able
to take better care of his family.

"But when he came back from the war, he was tired and sick.

"All night long the family
could hear him coughing
and talking feverishly.

Then once again he sat before a pile of
worn-out shoes.

"In his dreams he was often back in the war. For nights on end he had to march through ice and snow. 'I can see the Ice Maiden now!' he said one night. 'She's coming to get me.'

"Not long afterward he died.

"Hans was eleven years old. He went to a school for the poor.
His mother and grandmother had hardly any money at all."

"That's a sad story,"
said Elsa.
"Did Hans have any nice
things in his life?"

"Oh yes," said the man. "In fact, something really and truly wonderful. When he was fourteen years old,
the Royal Danish Theatre came from Copenhagen to put on a show in the town where he lived.
Young Hans not only watched every performance with great excitement,
but he was also invited to join in and come onstage as a shepherd.
From that moment on he knew what he wanted to do. He wanted to sing and dance and be on the stage.
He was going to become an actor! And so he decided he would join the theater in Copenhagen.

"Everybody laughed at him. But nothing and nobody could put him off, and so in the end his mother gave in.

"With thirteen coins in his pocket and a small bundle on his back, young Hans set out for Copenhagen.
'I hope he'll come back safe and sound,' his mother prayed as he left.

"She didn't know then that one day her son would become famous, just as you often read in fairy tales:
A poor boy sets out. He has nothing except his clever brain and his good heart—

and he ends up winning a kingdom ...."

"So did Hans become a king?"
asked Elsa, wide-eyed.
The man smiled. "No and yes.
He sometimes felt as if he'd got himself a kingdom—
the kingdom of letters. He became a famous writer.
His mother was very proud of him, and his father
would have been proud as well."

Elsa thought about it for a moment or two.
"And how did Hans become famous?
He was just a poor boy all alone
in the big city."

The man nodded.
"That's a good question. How did he do it?
Well, Hans took a letter with him to deliver
to a well-known dancer at the Royal Theatre.
He was supposed to introduce himself to her.
And so he went to see her.

"Without even thinking about it, he simply started to sing
and dance in front of her out of the sheer pleasure of
performing. He pulled his hat off his head and danced
and sang and leaped all around her room.

"The famous dancer thought,
'Poor boy. He's not quite right in the head.'

"And so she sent him packing. With tears in his eyes, young Hans wandered through the city.

"But Hans wouldn't give up. Although he didn't even have an appointment, he went to see the director of the Royal Theatre. He simply rang the doorbell. The director was taken by surprise, but he was impressed by the youngster's courage. And so he allowed Hans to sing a few songs and recite some poems for him and his guests. They all listened, spellbound. And then Hans received a round of loud applause for his performance. He could scarcely believe his own ears. These fine ladies and gentlemen were applauding him! The director offered to have him trained free of charge, and Hans was so happy that he burst into tears. At last life was being kind to him!

"He rented a small,
cheap room to live in,
and a kind professor
collected some money for him.
He was able to live frugally
on this.

"But when Hans turned fifteen, his voice changed. It became deeper and rougher. His breaking voice had lost its beautiful tone. And so Hans had to seek his fortune some other way.

EL BLOT TIL LYST

"He wrote a short play and performed it in front of a small audience, using homemade puppets
as actors and actresses. A director who saw the show got him a job at the theater.
He was given small parts to play, and once he appeared as a kobold (a mischievous spirit) in a ballet.
He was overjoyed—he had his name in the program! And he was even allowed to take a bow on the stage!

"What Hans really enjoyed,
though, was writing.
The sheet of paper became his stage,
and on it—using nothing but his imagination—
all kinds of possible and impossible things
could happen.
Poems, stories, fairy tales, and plays
all flowed from his pen ....

"A theater director who took a liking to him became his second father and took care of him. Hans was sent to a good school and did not have to pay any tuition.
One day, the well-educated student Hans went home to see his mother, and everyone was very proud of him. The son of the poor cobbler was now being invited to the homes of lords and princes, and they all loved talking to him."

"I like the story much more now," said Elsa happily.

"Me too," said the man. "And this tale of a life gets even better!

"Later, Hans would write lots of books, and they made him well known. He traveled around and visited towns and countries he had always wanted to see. He met famous people who—like himself—loved literature, music, and theater. Soon he became a much-respected figure, just as famous as they."

KING FREDERIK VI   JENNY LIND   CHARLES DICKENS   BROTHERS GRIMM

Elsa sat quietly for a while, playing with her dress, which rustled softly.

"Please may I ask
you something?"
she said.

"Carry on,"
said the man.
"Don't be shy."

"This Hans," said Elsa. "It's you, isn't it? And there's something I'd like to know.
Do the stories you write have anything to do with you? Or do you just make them all up?"
"That's a good but difficult question," the man answered.
"Let me think about it for a moment or two."
The man gazed out of the window for a while. The coach bumped along a country road.

"Hm. I'd say that many of my tales are about me and my dreams....
In my story 'The Flying Trunk,' a little boy sits in a trunk and flies away.
When I was a child, I'd have loved to sit in my old trunk, taken off,
and flown away!

"There's also a story about a girl who is no bigger than a thumb,
which is why she's called Thumbelina. She's so tiny that her bed fits
into a nutshell. One day this little girl flies south on the back of a swallow, and
there she meets her fairy prince who is as small as she is....
When I was a child, I often felt as tiny and helpless as Thumbelina.
And I would have loved to fly south on the back of a swallow...."

"There's another story about a princess who is so sensitive
that when she goes to bed, she can feel a pea through several
mattresses. I must confess, I'm also very sensitive.
And so if I'm really honest, I'll have to say that
the princess on the pea is a bit like me as well."

"One of my stories, 'The Ugly Duckling,' is about a duckling
who looks so different that all the other ducks make fun of him.
But one day the little duckling turns into a beautiful swan....
Anyone can turn into something special—that's what the story tells us.
Like a poor cobbler's son becoming a famous writer.

"In my story 'Clumsy Hans,'
a simple soul wins the heart of the king's daughter
just because he's clever and witty.
Language and humor—those are his riches!

"But I don't think my stories are all about me. With fairy tales you can sometimes hold a mirror out in front of other people without them realizing it.

"On my travels I've often come across people who think they're especially clever or posh, whereas in fact they're often just liars and flatterers trying to worm their way into the favor of princes and kings.

"In my story 'The Emperor's New Clothes,'
the emperor is given a new suit that apparently
can only be seen by people who are not stupid.
But there is no such suit. The emperor is naked!
Of course nobody wants to admit that they can't see the suit
because that would mean admitting that they're stupid.
And so the nonexistent clothes are praised and admired.
The emperor hears all kinds of magnificent lies....
It's only children who are clever
and honest enough to tell the truth.

"And I remember another story.
'The Snow Queen' is about someone
with a heart of ice.
Every now and then I've met people
like that whose hearts are frozen.
Fortunately, in my fairy tale
there are magic powers that can bring
such icy hearts back to life."

"Magic powers are good," said Elsa. "Can you do magic as well? If you can tell fairy tales, you must be able to do magic too.

"Isn't that right?"

"I think so," said the man with a vigorous nod.
"Or at least one must try. So, what magic would you like me to do?"
"The journey is taking far too long. I don't want to have to keep sitting in the coach. I'm aching all over. I'd like to be in Copenhagen right now! Can you magic the coach into flying? Like the flying trunk in your fairy tale?"
The man scratched his head thoughtfully.
"A trunk is smaller than a coach.
But we can try.
We must all hold hands.
Then each of us should
think of a magic word
without saying it.
We can say it to ourselves,
but only in our minds.
Are you all ready?"
Elsa, her mother, and the man
took one another's hands.
"Now close your eyes and think
of the magic word," whispered
the man.
There was a hushed silence inside
the coach.

One could hear the horses snorting outside, and the
clattering of the hooves and the rumbling of the wheels.
Suddenly a slight movement went through
the coach like a gust of wind.
Something gently raised the coach up in the air.

"Fly to Copenhagen!"
cried a cheerful voice.
There was the sound of
someone quietly laughing, and then the coach
soared silently up and away.

AUTHOR'S NOTE

Hans Christian Andersen was born on April 2, 1805, in Odense, Denmark.
Odense is the capital of Fünen, which is the second largest island in Denmark.
Hans left his hometown in 1819, at the age of fourteen, and in due course began to
make a reputation through his poems, stories, and plays.

His early journeys took him not only around his home country of Denmark,
but also to Germany, Italy, and France. Throughout his life he was a keen traveler,
and he visited many countries, initially by stagecoach and later by train.
He once said, "Travel means living."

His first original *Fairy Tales for Children* appeared in 1835 under the name of
H. C. Andersen—which was the name he used for all his books. In quick succession
he published fairy tales such as "The Tinder Box," "The Princess and the Pea,"
"The Emperor's New Clothes," "The Constant Tin Soldier," "The Flying Trunk,"
"The Wild Swans," "The Ugly Duckling," and "The Snow Queen."

Today these and many other tales by Andersen are among the treasures of
world literature.

In 1855 he published a memoir of his childhood entitled *The Fairy Tale of My Life*.
As an author, Andersen was a great success, but his private life was always unsettled.
He often moved, traveled a great deal, and never had a family of his own.
He spent his final years—much respected and honored, but also lonely—living alone
in Copenhagen.

On August 4, 1875, a few months after his seventieth birthday, Andersen died
at the family home of some friends in a suburb of Copenhagen.
Today one can see a statue of him in the Danish capital's City Hall Square.
A bronze statue of the Little Mermaid sitting on a rock in the harbor has
become the city's emblem. The figure is taken from one of his best-known stories,
and there are many other monuments to this famous Danish author.

April 2, his birthday, is celebrated as Hans Christian Andersen Day, when many towns
hold readings and literary events connected with books for children and young adults.
Every two years, the Hans Christian Andersen Award is presented to an author and an

illustrator of children's books in recognition of their life's work.
This award has long been regarded as the Nobel Prize for Children's Literature.
It is made by IBBY—short for International Board on Books for Young People—
which is an international organization that covers seventy-six different countries.
There is also an international Hans Christian Andersen Literature Prize that is
awarded every two years by a committee from Odense, Hans's birthplace.
His name lives on.

But it is above all his fairy tales that have immortalized his name.
On his many journeys, he was always accompanied by an old trunk.
There are photographs of the room in which he died, and one can see
the trunk on a chair next to his bed—ready for the last great journey....

It is also a reminder of his fairy tale "The Flying Trunk," in which a boy sits in
the trunk before starting out on a remarkable journey:
"It was a magic trunk. As soon as the lock was pressed, the trunk could fly.
The boy pressed it, and—whoosh!-the trunk flew, with him in it, up the chimney
and above the clouds, on and on, higher and higher....
The flying trunk is still high up there in the sky.
With every book we read and with every story we hear, the trunk swings open
and takes us on a magic journey....

HEINZ JANISCH was born in Güssing, Austria. He studied German and journalism in Vienna. He has worked for Austrian radio since 1982 and is editor of the series Menschenbilder [Human Images]. He has published countless books for children of all ages and has been awarded many prizes, including the Austrian Prize for Books for Children and Young Adults, and the Bologna Ragazzi Award. He has also been nominated for the German Prize for Children's Literature. Heinz now lives in Vienna and in Burgenland.

MAJA KASTELIC was born in Slovenia, where she studied painting, philosophy, and visual art theory. For several years she worked as a fresco restorer before devoting herself to illustrating children's books. Prizes include the White Ravens Award, and her work has been displayed at the Illustrators' Exhibition in Bologna.

In the illustrations for this book, there are references to well-known authors of children's literature.
Some famous children's book characters also crept in. They are a tribute to the creators of children's book classics.

First published in the United States, Great Britain, Canada, Australia, and New Zealand in 2020 by NorthSouth Books, Inc.,
an imprint of NordSüd Verlag AG, CH-8050 Zürich, Switzerland.

Distributed in the United States by NorthSouth Books, Inc., New York 10016.

Library of Congress Cataloging-in-Publication Data is available.
ISBN: 978-0-7358-4388-2
Printed in Livonia Print, Riga, Latvia, 2019
1 3 5 7 9 • 10 8 6 4 2